galway: city of strangers

VOICES OF THE NEW GALWAY

EDITED BY MICHAEL O'LOUGHLIN

*For Joe & Dora,
Old Galwegians
with an eye to the
future —
Michael O'L*

GALWAY CITY COUNCIL
ARTS OFFICE

Civic, 2008

GALWAY CITY COUNCIL ARTS OFFICE

First published in April 2008

Individual contributions © each author 2008
Collection © Galway City Council Arts Office, 2008

ISBN: 978-0-9559126-0-3
Title: Galway: City of Strangers
Format: 233mm x 158mm

Designed by Design Associates, Galway
Printed by Castle Print, Galway

CONTENTS

ACKNOWLEDGEMENTS

Special thanks to James Harrold of Galway City Arts Office, who godfathered this project from start to finish, and to Michael Burke, most literate of mandarins, of Galway City Council for his unstinting support, and Martha and Kathleen and all the staff at City Hall. To Donna, Fiona and Ann at IILT Galway for patience and dedication. To Brian MacNamara and Sean agus Nua for expert advice. To Siobhan and all the staff at Ballybane Library as well as the ladies of the Ballybane Writers' Group for many a memorable Friday morning. To Denise and Tommy at the Ballybane Resource Centre. Also, Marilyn Gaughan (Galway County Arts Office), Dolores Lyne, Pat McMahon, Magda Szulc, Seamus Sheridan, Jimmy and Matt at Tigh Neachtain, Páraic Breathnach and the Cúirt team, Helen Carey, Maura Kennedy, Sealines, Culture Ireland, Monica Corcoran (Head of Regions, The Arts Council), Charlotte Mangan, Vinny Browne, Gerry Hanberry, Fred Johnston, Kevin Higgins, Margaret Nolan, Galway Rowing Club, Breandán Ó hEaghra, Paul Callanan.

PREFACE

Galway is proud to call itself the City of Equals. We take great pride in our Anti-Racism strategy; we are an intercultural city and actively promote understanding and respect among the communities which make up our city. One way of so doing is through projects like this wonderful anthology, which allow the communities of Old Galwegians and New Galwegians to make their voices heard. Listening to each others' stories promotes mutual appreciation, and makes us more aware of our common identity as Galwegians, enabling us to treat each other with respect, equality and dignity.

Cllr Tom Costello, Mayor of Galway City

INTRODUCTION

Louis MacNeice called Galway 'the strangest town in Ireland', and I see no reason to disagree with him. When I arrived as a stranger in Galway at the end of 2006, I carried with me the usual preconceptions. Galway, to me, was the ultimate Irish town, less scarred by the Anglicisation of hundreds of years of English rule than the Anglophile East Coast. It seemed to be still in touch with the ancient traditions, with Irish murmured in the dark corners of its pubs, the Aran Islands floating strategically nearby, its streets haunted by the spirit of Yeats and Lady Gregory, the Moon Rising over the Spanish Arch. This was the soft, mystical West that James Joyce had headed East to get away from, though bringing it along with him in the beguiling form of Nora Barnacle. And in the course of the last century it had evolved into a fun town, a party town, famous for its traditional Irish music, its festivals, its cultural life.

The city I found was both more complex and more surprising than this. Certainly Galway is the most `Irish' of towns. But Irish in a definition far removed from the nationalist pieties of the cultural revolution which resulted in the Easter Rising in 1916 and the foundation of the Irish Free State in 1922.

Galway now seems to me a town characterised by ambiguities, reversals, transformations and a peculiarly split personality. But how I came to this conclusion is the story of this book.

My initial impression of Galway was unexpected: I was overwhelmed by the large amount of non-Irish nationals in this most Irish of cities. Everywhere you looked, you saw people who were obviously not born in this country. On the streets, in the bars and shops, you heard a cacophony of languages. As Magdalena Szulc, one of the contributors to this book points out, Galway is like a new Babel, hopefully one which will survive. People jokingly remarked to me that Irish speakers here were now outnumbered by at least half a dozen other languages, such as Polish, Russian, Chinese and so on. This is true, but Galway, like the rest of the country, has given little thought to the long-term cultural and political implications of this unanticipated but undeniable fact. In a way it is still too large to comprehend, blocking out the light.

After these initial impressions, I began to learn more about the history of the city. There were many unexpected facts. Of course, Galway the most Irish of cities, owed its building and prosperity to a wave of immigration, the Normans who came from France, and England. In the middle ages, these French-speaking immigrants turned Galway into a prosperous town. As you wander around the centre of Galway, there are moments when you get that familiar sensation, so typical of medieval trading cities. It reminds of me of corners of Amsterdam, of Riga, of Venice. European cities build on the sea, cities where politics, spirituality and culture always came second to their primary mission: commerce. Galway was part of that huge maritime superhighway which linked the world in a pre-globalisation network of trade. Galway has always been a cosmopolitan city. And it has always been about money: in present-day Galway you do not need to scratch under the surface very deeply to find this.

It is from those people, these Hiberno-Norman families, that Galway takes it title as 'The City of the Tribes'. This brand name was originally a term of scorn flung by Cromwellian invaders in the 17th century. That it has been embraced as a brand name is a typical example of Galwegian reversal. This city which banned Os and Macs from its streets, is now ruled by them. The New Galwegians become the Old Galwegians. Nothing is constant in Galway except change.

An example is the old Galway Gaol which had long loomed over many streetscapes. Deliberately so, a symbol and reminder of the absolute power of the British Empire's rule over the people of the West. Its shadow is still there, brilliantly made concrete some years ago in a work by Galway artist Louise Manifold. In a typical Galway festival of reversal, the space of the jail is now occupied by the Cathedral, in a certain light it still casts a very dark, ambiguous shadow. Also typical of the city, urban myth has it that the Cathedral includes in its body some of the stone plundered from the ruins of Coole Park. The fact that one of the historic cradles of genius, which witnessed the creation of many of Yeats' great poems, not to mention its association with

Lady Gregory, Synge and O'Casey, could be so casually destroyed is an indication of an Oedipal rage close to the surface. Few places I have encountered have such a strange relationship to their own past.

So, it occurred to me that Galway was above all, a City of Strangers. And I wanted to know how this city appeared to these new Tribes. So I embarked on this project. I invited people to contribute a short piece of prose or a poem about their experience of Galway. The aim was to hold a mirror up to present-day Galway, as seen by the New Galwegians. I wanted to compile a portrait of the city written not just by professional writers, but by the immigrant students and workers in the service industries, by the political refugees and asylum-seekers, who are only starting to learn English. But as I got to know Galway better, I began to realise that there were other dimensions to the concept of Galway as a City of Strangers.

It has often been remarked that the Irish should have been well adapted to the wave of immigration, as we ourselves are an emigrant nation. Yet somehow we never really quite made the connection. Working with writers' groups in Galway communities I soon became aware of something: that a large proportion of the population of native Galwegians, who were over the age of 60, had experienced emigration in the lean years of the 50s and 60s, mainly to Dublin, England, the USA and Canada. Obviously, they had returned. As a returned emigrant myself, I was well aware that once you leave, you will return as a stranger. So this group too were citizens of the City of Strangers. And then I began to realise that another large group of Strangers in Galway were the Irish themselves, most of whom seemed to come from outside the city, from places like Mayo, Dublin, and so on. And no one is as foreign in Galway as a Dubliner!

The results, the writings of the New Galwegians which appear in this book, in many ways surprised, shocked and moved me. Happily, they in no way matched my expectations. The Irish tend to look upon emigration as a banishment, an exile, a humiliation, an historical wound to be brooded upon. So I was surprised and vaguely disappointed perhaps, that so many of the contributors to this book look upon immigration into Galway as a positive experience. For young people from abroad in particular, it seems to be free of the traumas of displacement and social exclusion. They see only the positive aspects of their move here. In their eyes, Galway is a beautiful city magnificently situated on the ocean. The pubs are full of great music. The people are welcoming, friendly and open. We native Irish are often focused on the negative aspects of our medical, educational and civil service sectors. Yet many of the New Galwegians mention, and seem surprised by, the fairness, and compassion they experience in their dealings with official Ireland, often in stark contrast to their countries of origin. This is heartwarming for many of us, to see that the best of the old Irish values of community and hospitality have somehow survived the economic boom, even if they are not always visible.

The negative aspects touched upon in these writings are probably more predictable. The weather of course, particularly the horizontal rain which is a Galway speciality. And also the teenage drinking which leads to mayhem on the streets, something which shocks so many new arrivals. Irish cuisine gets a few disparaging mentions, though hopefully the New Galwegians will help to change that. New Galwegians are often surprised at how small Galway actually is. Also revealing, it seems that Galway's new tribes can jostle with each other as strongly as the old Tribes once did. Strangely and disappointingly to some people, few immigrants seem aware of or interested in the fact that some Old Galwegians speak a language which is not English.

The stories by returnees are eye-opening. Of course, returning is an unforgivable solecism, a fundamentally unpatriotic act. Behind it of course was the awareness that Ireland was unable to sustain its population. This was what independence had done for us. It was not always the brightest and best who stayed behind, but the ones best adapted to the new regime. And when they returned in the 1960s, they found a city where piped water and electricity were still considered exciting novelties. These are stories which the New Galwegians will find hard to believe. The twintub, a laborious way of washing clothes, could be a symbol of that era. The deficiencies of this Galway of the 70s and 80s were glaringly obvious to another subset of the returned immigrants: the children of Irish parents, born in the Diaspora.

They returned not to claim their birthright, but to cash the cheque accumulated by their parents' exile. They are rarely if ever satisfied with the rate of exchange.

Interestingly, the writings by the Irish 'Strangers' and English-langage immigrants are both more ambiguous and more passionate about Galway. They seem acutely aware of the other half of Galway's cosmopolitan personality, the tensions beneath the famous 'buzz', the small town jealousy, conservatism, and stultification. As the American Quincy Lehr illustrates in his witty piece, Galway is the victim of its own success. Galway has brilliantly sold itself as Ireland's Cultural Capital. But now that the world is coming to Galway, its cultural infrastructure has been shown to be remarkably underfunded and underdeveloped. Hopefully, this will change. The town will have to pay for the city.

Above all, the picture that emerges from these writings is of a vibrant, open city, full of contradictions but alive and unpredictable. Twenty five years ago, in the particularly grim period that was Ireland in the early 1980s, it would have been interesting to ask people to make predictions about life in Ireland 25 years later. I doubt if any of them would have even come close to the constantly surprising, fascinating and strange Ireland we now live in. To paraphrase Yeats, this is not the dead Ireland of my youth, but an Ireland the poets dreamt of, terrible and gay. Soon, we will have children born here, raised speaking Irish and Polish, or English and Latvian, who will start to write their own stories. They will create their own narratives, their own Irish tradition. This book aims to give a picture of Galway as it now is, and was in the recent past. Above all, I hope you will catch a glimpse of the Galway which does not yet exist.

Michael O'Loughlin, Galway, April 2008

galway: city of strangers

"Salmon in the Corrib
Gently swaying
And the water combed out
Over the weir
And a hundred swans
Dreaming on the harbour...'

Louis MacNeice

I'M NOT IRISH, I'M FROM KERRY...

Driving home from work the other day I couldn't help noticing the change in the driving culture on the roads of Galway. I remember that some years ago, first time in Galway or in Ireland in general, I was surprised when cars stopped for me when as a pedestrian I tried to cross the road, or when driving, and at one of those annoyingly narrow but still two-lane streets I tried to make a turn and suffered for minutes well expecting the others to wish me to hell aloud but still all they did was patiently stop and try to give me as much space as possible. I couldn't believe it. I was used to the impatience and aggression of car drivers of my homeland.

Well, times are changing. These days cars are running much faster and less and less politely on the streets of Galway too. I hate to admit it but we, foreign drivers are at least partly guilty of this sin...

Never mind. Still driving and giving the usual ride to a Polish colleague of mine whom I happened to know from my time in the US before, and we were talking about Romania and Bulgaria joining the EU. He was pissed a bit and said: *'We shouldn't let them come. They will work for 3-4 Euro per hour and will take our jobs sooner or later.'* I just looked at him, speechless, and I couldn't believe the situation...

I might be an *auslander* but I like to have my Guinness in the pub when it is raining outside. Yeah, I know it is a cheap excuse to put the blame on the weather but still, I am sure the success of Irish pubs owes a lot to the Irish rain. I took a cab on the way home, and started to explain the route to the driver who happened to be a black guy. I guess it was obvious from my accent that I was born in a faraway place too, 'cos he asked me straight away: *'Are you a Polak?'* I was drunk enough to have a conversation about it, so I said: *'Who? Me? Do I look like one? Come on man, I am not blond, I am not blue-eyed and I am not handsome. I am a Bloody Hungarian, why?'* *'Good, because there are too many Polish people around in town. They take the jobs from us.'* I just had to ask him about his origins. *'I have been living here for seven years, I am Irish...'*

Walking home again after a long and hard day's work in town. A colleague of mine walks next to me because we live close to each other. It is a Saturday night, well after midnight with loads of drunk youngsters rampaging on the streets. All we can hear is some drunk voices insulting us from behind: *'Look at those two bald gay weirdoes! Why don't you grab each others' hands and sing like real homos?'* My friend mumbled back something to give them an excuse to continue: *'Fucking Eastern Europeans, Hitler didn't do a good job on you. Go home and don't poison the air here.'* Not just for old times sake, but I couldn't help laughing out loud while showing a tattooed swastika on my body to them. *'You wanna teach me about hatred, mon ami? My grandfather was a Waffen SS officer. Try harder.'* I guess the sight was enough and there was no need to tell them that the Hungarian was the only Axis army on the Russian Front with numerous Jewish officers, or that the Hungarian nation sent more Hungarian nationals of Jewish origin to Auschwitz in one month than other countries in years. Even the Gestapo officials were surprised how much we could hate our own.

The drunk youngsters left us alone that night. I didn't have the chance to tell them that I had been a firm believer in far right radical politics back home, seen so much aggression and hatred that most folks would hardly see it in several lifetimes and now I am a foreign guest worker in a country thousands of miles away from the place we once called the motherland which we wanted to defend from the outsiders. Life has a wicked sense of humour I guess...

Years ago, when I got to Ireland after same traveling in other parts of the world, I had some hard times, like most of us immigrants, I guess. Finally I met this guy who helped me in a lot of things, and asked for nothing in return. He had an interesting past too, although mainly on the streets of Killarney, Cork and finally Galway. I was surprised that as an Irish person, he wasted so much time and energy on me, the foreigner. He told me that it is because I proved to him that there is a way back to society for everyone. I proved to him that it can be done. He also said that he *is not Irish, he is from Kerry*...

Frank, Hungary

IS GALWAY THE OPPOSITE OF THE TOWER OF BABEL?

What comes to mind upon hearing the phrase the Tower of Babel? Confusion? Scattering? Variety? Babel WAS a cosmopolitan city characterized by a confusion of languages. And Galway? Galway IS a cosmopolitan city. Can we say it is characterized by a confusion of languages? We certainly can, but there's more to it than just a surface-deep observation.

Galway is the Tower of Babel standing on its head. According to the biblical account, Babel was a city that united humanity, all speaking the same language and migrating from the East. Isn't Galway a city that unites humanity? Don't we all have to speak one (English) language in order to communicate? Haven't a lot of us migrated here from the East? It's all true, however, the reason Babel was built in the first place was to unite people of various backgrounds and it ended in all those people being scattered all over the world. Galway, on the other hand, was, up to a few years back with, with only some exceptions, a town full of the native inhabitants of Ireland: the Irish. Over the past several years, it has been transformed into a place inhabited by all those, previously scattered all over the globe or other parts of the Emerald Isle.

The people of Babel decided that the city should have a colossal tower reaching to the sky, having "its top in the heavens." However, the tower was built for the wrong reasons. Instead of worshipping God, people working on it wanted to make a good name for themselves. God decided to punish them by confusing their languages and scattering them throughout the earth.

Galway, in contrast, keeps attracting more and more stray, confused people, as if God was doing his unscattering , flocking his herd of lost sheep back together, in a different time and a different location. Instead of our numerous languages expanding and people, against their will, being made to speak in different tongues, a completely reverse process is taking place.

We're constantly congregating in our Babel city of Galway and willingly aiming at communicating in one language. We know we wouldn't be able to otherwise, however doing so isn't against our will, and nobody is making us get rid of our native tongues.

Could what's happening mean we're getting back into God's good books? Is God trying us out in different circumstances? This type of reasoning could certainly appeal to Christians. Have we, though, really displayed reasons to deserve such treatment? There are cases of open, unconcealed abhorrence towards people of different nationalities to those who offend, for no reason whatsoever. Luckily, with the overwhelming majority blending in well with the rest of the city's population, we certainly are on a good track. Perhaps we should treat it as an encouraging factor towards appreciation of what a great place we inhabit and learn to respect others who share this melting pot with us. Unlike those builders who neglected what the real reason for building the tower should have been, let us constantly be in awe of the blessing that being a part of this city's abundant culture truly is.

Magdalena Szulc, Poland

DAISY

I take up space
with my sun-freckled brow,
my fat French lips, my fat
American vowels –
"to-MAY-to,
a-LOO-min-um,
MAWL" –
my love bitten neck,
my big fat thighs, my
PERSONALITY
soft as the sheen of sweat.
I take up space, sip coffee.
The café is dead
at this hour, late sun captive
in glass.

They take up space
with their proper posture, shrill
lipstick, brittle
opinions propped up by
distinguished gentlemen,
distant or dead;
themselves propped up by
extinguished gentlemen,
fucked up or fled.

They take up space,
these women and their ghosts.
They summon the waitress,
sip tea,
glare at me.

They think I take up
too much space.
That I ruined
my husband, poor Irish lad –

and I have, it's true,
ruined him, like
a suburban lawn is ruined
by the daisy's
wide awake eye.

Susan Millar DuMars, USA

COMING BACK

When I reached my teenage years my desire to travel was great. I longed to get away from home, away from the routines and rules. I love my parents, brothers and sisetrs dearly but they suffocated me entirely. You had to face them each and every day. The younger ones, you had to help take care of and then there was Dad. He exercised his authority over us kids and Mum. I hated seeing him discipline my brothers. Well, they were allowed physical punishment back in the 1960s when I began my teenage years. Mum had to have dinner on the table when Dad came home from work. I know he worked very hard; abattoir work was not the easiest of tasks back then.

Nowadays everything is done by electricity. He had to use his stamina, back-breaking work. He was tired and hungry, I can understand that, but Mum worked too looking after us. I guess I just did not understand family life.

I had no idea where I wanted to go. America, perhaps, I could go over to my aunts in New York. Mum did not want me to leave home at all so I had to plan my escape. It would not be easy because my sister had already left and she needed me to help her. I decided Dublin City would be my best bet, that way I would be away from home but yet not so far away, I could still lend a hand.

So I studied hard and got work in Dublin City. It was a great sense of relief to leave it all behind and build my own future far away from home i.e. Galway. I spent 13 years in Dublin. In the beginning it was pure bliss. I forgot about Galway, my school friends, neighbours, but I could not forget my family. I began to miss them incredibly. I missed the familiar faces in a crowd, and loneliness set in. I missed the nearness of places like the cinema or shopping centres or just the town. I needed to go home again.

So I packed my bags and my family and went back to live in Galway again. At first, it was great to be back with the people I missed and loved, but Galway had changed and mostly my friends, neighbours and family had changed. They had done what I did, set about making their own space, i.e. set up a family of their own. They had grown up in 13 years. My little brothers were no longer little and I was not their big sister either. I was Kevin's wife and mother to my own kids. They no longer needed me to help them grow up. They did that without me. Now I was just the visitor, the sister who left home. Why, they wondered, had she come back?

When I would go down the town nobody recognised me and I only recognised a few. We had all changed in appearances and attitudes to one another. I felt I had to start all over again and build up what I had left behind. But it was too much trouble, too much of a task. Only time could do that for me, to reacquaint myself with everyone and everything.

I felt I was away too long to ever come back. I was a stranger again. People did not recognise me. Galway too was changed, more new housing estates and factories were built where we used to play hide and seek in the long grass. My favourite places were hidden by new buildings. Everything dear became just a memory. I spent my years telling my children about the loves of my youth. It took them a long time to settle into Galway. It took me time too.

I felt the familiar feeling of routines and rules set in, only this time I set the rules and routines. My children struggled with them too. Some of them left home and some did not. I know now how they feel. Going away from home is everyone's desire and right. Exploring new friends and places is normal. Coming back again is not, because it is never the same place as before. People change and grow up.

Life is full of surprises!

I remember the rambling rose bush that climbed around the gable door. Red roses so sweet. The primroses that flocked against the stone walls. Now all gone.

Torn down and tread upon. Great big steel buildings lay where once we played and had fun. Now all gone.

Lilly Mooney, Galway

GALWAY

I came to Ireland in 1991. I lived in Dublin when I arrived. Then I moved to Galway after a year in 1992.

The first time I saw Galway I was shocked. I found Galway to be a small city. It was different to Dublin. I felt that there weren't many people here. There was no traffic and it was a very quiet city. There weren't many shops in town like now. There were many cows and sheep on the streets.

There weren't many foreign people living here. But nowadays there are a lot of foreign people working and living here. The Irish people in Galway are friendly and nice but they are private people.

Galway is the birthplace of my children. I like Galway. I always tell my friends Galway is the best place in the world. Now I feel sad because I'm going to leave Galway this summer.

Kheiria El-Gamiti, Libya

COMING TO IRELAND

Well, where do I start? I was saving this information for my autobiography.

I'll never forget the day I came to Ireland. It was in March 1990 and the weather was fine. I know what you're thinking. That's not usually the case in Ireland. My journey was very last minute and not very well planned. I only intended to go to Ireland for a three week holiday, but this holiday turned into what now feels like a life time.

I packed my large suitcase quickly and told my three house mates that I had decided to go on holiday. They were a bit shocked as I hadn't mentioned Ireland to them before. They knew why I was going. It was to be with my Irish boyfriend because I missed him very much.

My sister and the rest of my family thought I was completely mad. They believed what they saw on the news which gave an impression of Ireland as a place where bombs were going off all the time.

I took the ferry from Holyhead to Rosslare. My journey was an exciting new adventure for me. I talked to lots of different people who were making the same journey. Most of the people I chatted to asked me the same question, "Why are you going to Ireland?" I would later came to understand why...

The train journey from Heuston seemed to last forever, but thank God there was a lovely old lady who sat next to me. We chatted and laughed most of the way until she got off at the stop before Athenry. I looked out of the window to pass the time and soon realised I was in the countryside now. It wasn't long before I realised why people were so surprised at my journey to a small town in the west of Ireland. I became very nervous. They weren't many foreigners in Ireland nineteen years ago.

In fact I was the first black person to ever live in the town.

I'm so glad that I have made Ireland my home. I have studied, had my children and worked here. I will probably move on and retire in a new country, but for now Ireland is my home.

Anonymous, Jamaica/England

THE "BUZZ" IN GALWAY

Galway is a small city where everyone bumps into the same people again and again. It is probably one of the main reasons why so many people find it easy to call it home, even if they are not native Galwegians. If I could make a list of all the people I have met in the last six years, I would probably come up with nearly five hundred names! Actually, this is not quite true, because I would have no idea what half of their names are. You might call them "Hi-friends": people you keep meeting in the same places, and who have become familiar faces. Whether it is walking down Shop Street or taking a stroll on the promenade, most people look at each other and smile as they pass; they acknowledge each other, unlike Paris, London or other big cities, where everyone is in such a hurry that all they look at is their own feet. I feel very much alive in Galway and the whole city is filled with enthusiasm; I often hear folks say that Galway has a "great buzz". It could be because this positive energy comes from the fact that every individual is happy to walk around in such a friendly environment, whether they are locals, students, tourists, or the likes of myself: foreigners but not quite strangers to Galway anymore!

People are generally friendly and easy to talk to. This is lovely and it really increases a sense of community. However, although they don't mean to, these same people also remind me that I am not from here, all the time. In every single conversation I have with someone I have just met, I am always asked three questions: "Where are you from?"; "How long have you been here?"; "What brought you here?". This can be a bit irritating sometimes! Once I decided to try the same thing, so I asked this guy from Sligo where was he from himself. He was very surprised! But why should I have to justify my situation more than anyone else does? And how many more times will I hear "Where is this lovely accent from?" and "Where exactly in France are you from?" I suppose I know the answer: I will hear these same comments over and over again for as long as I live here!

Anyway, even if I am reminded how French I am a bit more often than I would like, I still consider Galway my home. And I don't know whether I adopted Galway or Galway adopted me, but here I am now. When I first came to Ireland nearly ten years ago, I intended to stay for two months to improve my English. Now, my English is fine, and I can speak a few words of Irish, Spanish and Italian, I can play a few Swedish tunes and I can cook Japanese rice as well! In a wonderful way, Galway and its people manage the paradox of keeping the Irish tradition alive while welcoming all the strangers who pass by for a few months – as well as the one who never leave!

Marie Robineau, France

GALWAY

I came to Galway in July 2001. Before I came to Galway, I decided to choose between Galway and Letterkenny. I went to Letterkenny first to visit and I came to Galway also to visit.

The way I saw it in Galway was that, the people were friendly people. If you go to hospital any where you go, you can be satisfied that they are good people, especially IILT teachers and my computer teacher. Everyone was also nice to anybody.

I started this school last year June 2007. I can say that, I speak better English than before because I couldn't speak English at all. So now I can go to anywhere I want to go. I thank IILT English and computer school. Now I speak by myself. Before, my husband was the one that talk for me but now I talk for myself. IILT teachers in Galway, God will bless them in Jesus name, Amen.

Anonymous, Ghana

GALWAY

While Galway swells both
sides of the stony Corrib,
her macaronic voice echoes
with car-horn, horse hoof and
the tok-tok of harbour boats,
drunk with Spanish sailors.

All the air is fish-reeky where
Nimmo's Pier points a long
lazy arm to Black Head,
and the suck of the sea
pulls the eye to Salthill,
soaked under April storms.

Skirling origami swans decorate
the Claddagh basin while Galway
settles her night-shawl down,
boats and birds safe at her breast.
And her poets – all of her poets –
are upfront about love.

Nuala Ní Chonchúir, Dublin

COMING TO GALWAY

My first job in Ireland was in a place called Maam Cross, not far to Galway. I worked in a pub there. The nature was very beautiful but I had a big problem. Most people in the pub were old men and they were very difficult to understand. I studied English at home but I couldn't understand what they said. This often made them angry. Also the work was very hard and not interesting. I was not happy.

My friend asked to come to Galway to work with her in a café. This is much better for me now. In the summertime, there are a lot of tourists. That is good for us, because tourist are very good tippers. The Irish, not so much!

I live in an apartment with four other girls from Slovakia, we have a good time. There is a bar in Salthill where we go all the time. People come there not just from Slovakia but countries like Poland and Lithuania as well. It's a great place to have fun and party, and to meet other people from many countries. Galway is a small place but I think there is people here every country in Europe. You can see that in all the shops, with special foods, for Poles, Russians, and the Africa countries.

Ireland reminds me a lot of Slovakia. The people are friendly and make you welcome. If I am not working I like to just walk around the streets and look at people, there is always something happening. Also, there is a great market on Saturdays, you can buy food fresh from the farmers, that is like home too. I have some Irish friends too, I think people here are eager to make friends with you.

One thing I don't like in Galway is when people ask me where I'm from. If I say Slovakia, they always think that is part of Yugoslavia! I don't think I will stay in Galway. I want to study, I am interested in studying sculpture because art is my hobby. But it is easier to study in Bratislava than here. I see a lot of students working in the café, they are always tired, and it's hard for them here. I am now saving money, so that I can go back and study and not worry about money. Most people I know do not stay here. They work for some years and then go back to their country. I know that someday I will do the same. But I will never forget Galway, the good times I have here.

I know that after I go, I will always return. Galway is in my blood now.

Lenka, Slovakia

NOTES ON HOMECOMING

The temperature has always been higher at my departures than it was at my homecomings. This is linked to the great expectations on my leaving which makes my homecomings an anticlimax.

Although I have never been away from this country for more than eighteen months, I have experienced three notable homecomings.

I emigrated to Montreal, Canada in 1958, a month or so after leaving school. Initially I stayed with relatives, but as soon as I got my bearings I branched out on my own. At first I stayed in a hostel for young ladies in the centre of Montreal. Later I moved to Toronto where I got myself a bed-sit or a studio apartment as they later called it there.

However I never really settled in Canada, I found the summers far too humid and the cold, cold winters with snow from November to April, too much to bear what with me coming from a more temperate climate. But I was glad of the opportunity to broaden my horizons.

I had the rare experience of cruising home to Ireland on a fabulous Cunard Liner called the Carinthia, boarding at Halifax, Nova Scotia and arriving in Cobh, Co. Cork, six days later.

Because I had only been away something short of two years, not a lot had changed in Galway. I had.

I am told that I had a North American accent though I couldn't hear it. I loved being back in the old familiar haunts. Walking down Shop Street shortly after my return I met an acquaintance of mine. 'I didn't see you for a while, were you away?', said she to me. Now to ask anyone in Galway 'were you away?' had a certain connotation, being away could mean you were in a mental institution, however, that conversation showed that I was hardly missed. What a welcome!

I stayed at home, for about nine months until I got restless again. The second homecoming was from Frankfurt-am-Main in 1961. I worked there as a chambermaid and at other times as a hotel laundry assistant. On arriving in Germany, apart from 'Guten Tag' and 'Auf Wiedersehen',

I couldn't speak a word of German. I very quickly acquired a working knowledge of German, as the people I worked with didn't speak English. Every now and then when I try my 'cúpla focal' it is often a German word that enters my mind first, and that after forty years!

'Did you like Germany?', they asked when I came home. I can still only praise German efficiency, you would never hear a German say 'Sure, it'll be grand'.

My last homecoming was from London in 1964. I think it was Samuel Johnson who said 'he who is tired of London is tired of life.' Whether that is true or untrue I do not know. I do know I was tired of wandering.

At my Wedding in 1965 my uncle, the local parish priest, said I had come home to roost.

Ida Greaney, Galway

HOW I CAME TO GALWAY

When I first came to Ireland in November 2000 it was difficult, I could not understand English. I started to learn a word a day. The weather is very different to my country I did not go out or leave the hostel because it was cold outside and I felt like I was inside a fridge.

In December 2000 I saw the snow it was the first time in all my life. I will not forget that day. I was very happy it was something different and new. I played like a kid. Outside I made a snow man, I had fun but after that came back to reality.

The Department of Justice sent me to Mayo. It was a small town named Ballycastle. There were only fifteen houses, two churches, two pubs and four cemeteries. During the day we only saw old people, but at night the pubs were full of young people and some of them stayed outside talking loudly. I heard them from my window. One time me and my husband went down to the pub in the hostel. It was one of only two pubs in the village and we were surprised to see many young people there. We asked ourselves where they came from as this town is small and empty during the day. It was strange because in Cuba, we see people at night and in the daytime.

Then we came to Galway. This is much better. There are many shops and places to go. I am happy here now.

Anonymous, Cuba

"BLOW-INS"

One of the truisms of Irish society, mentioned with great frequency on the public radio and with some regularity by weird geriatric types on public transportation, is that it is becoming more pluralistic, or at least that there are people about who don't look like the rest of us. And, given my own northern European descent and English being my native tongue, I tend to be more privy to the latter than the typical foreigner. I find myself, as an American living in Ireland, having to point out to certain Irish xenophobes, that I am a 'bloody foreigner', too. But that's a matter I'll leave aside for now, because one of the strange advantages of being foreign, but American, is that one pretty quickly moves in 'Irish' circles.

And it is to a large extent among the Irish population that one finds what makes Galway unusual for an Irish city of its size. Sitting in a pub in the city centre of Galway, one will not only hear the occasional American, English, Australian, or continental European accent, not to mention African or Asian ones—but also Cork accents, Kerry accents, and Dublin accents. And so forth. And in many ways, I find those accents more interesting than my own. In part, this may be because, after two years of living here, I find the tropes of foreignness a bit tedious by now, but it is also because the internal migration is not without its own significance.

The stories revolve around a theme that I can recall quite well from growing up in a college town in the United States. Someone shows up, visiting an old chum for a week. Galleries are visited; pints are downed; concerts are attended; kebabs of varying quality are consumed. He or she then sticks around, gets a job at a café, and gets really into writing or playing the guitar or smoking dope or riding the bike. Or whatever. And Galway, to many of these blow-ins seems like a good place to do it.

And Galway, for all the overheated real estate market and crap water supply and all, is a good little town for noodling around on the guitar or writing whatever the equivalent of the Great American Novel might be. Because—and here's the dirty little secret—there isn't that much to do in Galway. There isn't much in the way of cinema. And yes, there are pubs and clubs, but only a certain number of them. So, you drink heavily or you get involved in local theatre or you go out to poetry readings or you set up a gallery or try to get a job in one. And when your friends come in from Co. Longford or Dundalk or wherever, they're surprised at how much groovy stuff there is going on. And really, a lot of it seems to be a bunch of people from somewhere else trying to keep themselves entertained.

And you can't force that kind of thing. You can just hope that the rent stays cheap and the drug scene doesn't get too scary and that the beautiful woman visiting from Drogheda whom you know because she's crashing on a friend's couch until she 'gets her shit together' sticks around for a while. And in the interim, you can hang around in the pubs, listening to how people from just down the road, the other side of the island, or somewhere else entirely ended up here, often quite inadvertently, and show no signs of leaving anytime soon, and it is they, as much as anyone else, who make Galway what it is.

Quincy Lehr, USA

MY EXPERIENCE IN GALWAY

I'm a mother of four girls. My fourth daughter has some special needs. When we noticed her condition we told our G.P. who referred us to the hospital. She used to cry more than was normal. She could not explain what was wrong with her by this time she was three I noticed something was not right. I didn't know how to explain it. So the doctor in the hospital told me that she had global developmental delay.

They referred us to Fairlands Child Development Services.

The teachers there were was very concerned because of this situation. I was not feeling well I wanted to die my head was hot I was depressed when I slept last night I thought to myself this was a dream but when I woke up in the morning the dream was still there. One of her teachers noticed it and decided to speak with me. I told her I'm not feeling well.

Because of my daughter's situation she said to me, we know about her situation but what do you want us to do for you, she spoke to me as my mother or my sister. My daughter was then enrolled in Fairland's Early Childhood Development School. She has been attending the school since September 2007. She's much better now.

She is happy now especially when she is going to school on the school bus.

Edyth EhimareBrave, Nigeria

GASTARBEITERS

Allow for the fact that we were in this town for the first time
and that no one here takes us for locals and even automatic doors
(which register light particles) do not always open at our approach.
Remember how, not very long ago, dressed as sailor-boys,
crumpled, like the pages of damned-because-left-behind notebooks,
we stepped onto the readied aircraft steps, so we could without
looking at our fellow passengers' (their sighs of relief) sideways
glances, leave the plane for the first time, and then for ages couldn't
find the addresses we needed...
Remember that nobody met us, and even the dispatcher, (or whoever
it is, talking away to the whole airport), announced our flight, barely
restraining her laughter, as if she was being tickled by a team of
window cleaners...

And if I tell you how we randomly moved towards the town centre,
Trying not to attract attention, hiding stencils in our bags
(Such as we imagined every decent person owned),
And carrying with us very distinct plans for your town...
How we moved along walls, hiding in our bags those very same stencils,
Passing aerosol cans like relay runners... losing on our way (countless)
Meccano pieces from our favourite childhood box set....
How during the day we jumped up and down behind tourists having
their photos taken,
So we could land in their shots (appear in their albums) which we
Would never see – although by now there must be a good few of
them around.

And remember how innocently convinced we were that we
could earn a living
Dressed up as huge bunnies at childrens' parties or as
(no smaller, these)
Blow-up hot dogs on the paved areas in front of railway stations.

And, or so the tale went, one of us even gave lessons in Russian
orthodox aerobics...
And although (when the allocated time had run out) we still couldn't
tell noughts
From letter o's, and the automatic doors, to go back to them,
Would generally (as already stated) open only with reluctance, we still
Hoped somehow to get to grips and still maintained a grain of respect
for ourselves...

Enough to remember how we did meet with people
Who could have been useful and sorted us out, but there was
Too much noise, and all we could manage were a few friendly words
Motioning with the long throats of beer bottles (smiling over and over)
And even without words it was obvious that they could offer us
Nothing definite (at least not yet).
Although everyone hopes we are having
A marvellous time...
And it stuck in my mind how you suddenly
Said:

"It's fine. It isn't our style, rushing around. You'll find us later
On the town beach (nursing letters from home and an airhostess)
Where we went to fly a kite in farewell...
Aim for the marker – an orange cat in the blue sky.
And if anyone else is more in need than us, we can still collect a few
hundred – pay it back when you can.
Makes no odds, the coins over here (when we get back home) are only
really useful for tightening small screws.

Artur Punte, Latvia

FROM EAST TO WEST

I come to Ireland to study English. My city is called Dalian, in the north of China. In begin, I came to Dublin and I lived with a host family. The house was nice and the family was very kind. The food was strange. A lot of potatoes. But there are many Chinese in Dublin with many excellent Chinese restaurants. I studied English in a college and worked in the day. It was tiring. I lived with my friends in Bray and the bus from Dublin was long. One day me and my friend went to Galway for holiday. I like Galway very much. The people are friendly and polite, everyone says hello. I moved here to live with my friends.

For one month I lived in a house in a place in Galway outside the city. I go on the bus to work every day. When I come home the children follow me and shout and laugh and call me names. I don't understand that parents leave them do this. They pulled my clothes, very little children too! But they are joking.

It was hard to find work. I worked in a bar in Salthill. It was very hard. At weekends everyone was drunk, also girls. They drink a lot, like the men, and they are very loud, always shouting, so loud! They are fat. When the bar is closing they stand on the tables and sing and push me when I am picking up glasses. I was afraid. They wear too sexy clothes. I don't like it working in bar so I get a job in a supermarket. My boss is very kind and takes care of me. He invited me to a party in his house. His mother and wife were there, it was very nice. I danced with his mother. Now I am assistant manager.

The shops in Galway are good. When I have a day free, I like to shop with my friends. Brown Thomas is beautiful, lots of things like handbags and shoes. I go there but it is very expensive.

In Dublin there are many Chinese restaurants and shops, but only some in Galway. However, I have many friends here and we are happy. I don't like to go to pubs. We like sometimes to go to friends' house and cook a nice meal. We laugh a lot and talk. I like cooking but I have no time, I am too tired when work is finished. I often eat hamburgers,

I like that, but Chinese food is better and more healthy. I like fish and shellfish, that are expensive here too, I don't understand.

People in Galway always ask me the city I'm from, they don't know it. It has more people than Ireland! Ireland is very small, and Galway is very small, but I like it.

At Chinese New Year I go back to Dalian to be together with my family. My mother is sad that I am in Ireland. But I think I work here and learn English and earn money to save.

I like Galway very much. But China is my home. My family and friends are there. I will always go back to China, but now Galway is good.

Jenny, China

IMPRESSIONS OF GALWAY

As the train pulled into the station I noticed the name Ceannt Station and wondered what this city might hold for me. Eye specialist Mr. Ceannt had diagnosed a brian tumour earlier in my life and my eyes were again giving me lots of trouble although medics from the top down seemed to think there was nothing amiss.

I alighted from the train and was driven to Tirellan Heights, a nice sprawling estate on the edge of Galway City. After a lovely home-cooked meal I began to unpack and settle in.

A tour of the city showed it to be on the small side with lots of other estates and shopping centres off the centre, each a little world in its own right. As the locals say, 'Galway is a big town really.'

Galway has a large cross cultural mix and it's a bit unclear as to how welcome 'foreigners' are. Is it true to say that Galway dwellers are somewhat intolerant of people who do not exactly fit in?

I find Galway a very safe place indeed with almost no crime and when the law is broken the culprits are quickly brought to justice.

Shop staff seem to be out not 'to do you, make a quick buck', rather, they go out of their way to be helpful, and if they haven't got the required merchandise will quickly tell you where the same may be acquired.

However, Galway is on the expensive side. Goods that cost about 35 Euro here can be purchased for 27 Euro on the East Coast. When I said this to Mary, a Meath inhabitant, she explained that she believed this was always the case in 'these touristy places'.

Maybe that explains it, I don't know, but Galway certainly draws tourists from all over the world. No wonder, when it's so safe, and has so much to offer. The *Arts Festival* takes place over a fortnight, and has several culturally interesting events going on all over the place every day. Then there's Halloween, the Oyster Festival, St. Patrick's celebrations and other focal points dotted throughout the year and celebrated in Galway. All enhanced greatly by street theatre and the colour, spectacle and atmosphere engendered by Macnas.

Hettie, A Scottish friend of mine, her husband Rick and their teenagers Ian and Hannah spent a few days here recently. Booked into a local hostel they shared a room with four beds and an ensuite. Up the road they had fresh Irish stew at 10 PM and the landlord's children provided live céilí music all night. They were favourabley impressed!

Next day we were passing the Black Box Theatre where a dance troupe was performing nightly. Hettie explained that they wanted to 'see some real Irish dancing when in Galway'. In the Black Box ticket office the ticket seller listended as Hettie explained what she wanted and prepared to buy tickets for the show.

'Just a sec,' he said. 'This might not be the best place for what you want. There's a better show like you've described in Salthill at the moment.' He allowed her phone and book tickets for the show he recommended which was 'absolutely brilliant.' Only in Galway would you meet this kind of service.

On the East Coast I worked as journalist with some local papers. I wanted to break into more creative stuff but just didn't know how.

I came to Galway, joined a creative writing group and in no time was inspired not only to write creatively but to have a bash at my first book.

Not long after coming to Galway persistent eye infections saw the GP refer me to a young optician called Annie O'Sullivan, Galway Eye Clinic, Galway Shopping Centre. Within a few minutes she found out why I was having so much eye trouble, started treatment and got me dark glasses which have greatly helped. I know some other people who have had their eye problems eased in Glaway.

My impression of Galway? I'm impressed!

Sister Valerie Malone, Meath

TELLING STORIES

I came to Ireland on 1st March 2006. It was so amazing in my country on that day. It was snowing and when I came here everything was so green and alive with a little sunshine. My father met me, my mother and my brother at the airport. The house I went to live in was very nice. I went to see the city and for me, everything was so exciting and so new. People were different, they were spekaing in English. I wanted to understand them, but I couldn't at that moment. When I met teenagers they smiled and said hi to me.

First when I went to see the city I was lost. I walked a lot to find my way home. I walked for a long time. The city was extremely beautiful. I took a taxi. The taxi driver was a lovely person. He began to ask me questions. I tried to answer. He said 'Welcome to Ireland'. These words made me feel really good. I tried to be positive. I stayed at home for a month and I tried to learn on my own. Then I started an English course which helped me a lot. Everyday I learned something new in school. Was positive and I was eager to learn new things. I taught myself to be patient and to listen to people. I was quiet for some time. I felt like a small child. Then I started to understand a little, then more and more. Gradually I started to speak. I chatted to Irish people I tried to understand their jokes.

Once when I was walking on my way home a man stopped me and asked: 'When do you think is the best time to go to the market? I didn't know what to say. He smiled and said: 'When it's raining'. I smiled warmly. People here are so friendly they give you a friendly smile despite the difficulties of living nowadays.

When I go into the city I like to listen to music and how people sing. This music makes me feel alive.

Today I look at myself and I realise I've lived here for one year and three months. I remember all my first steps. I know the most important thing is to begin, start. Sometimes I thought I can't cope with it, but I kept thinking 'just begin'. It's the way to achieve something you really want. So I started and I try to do my best to learn, to help my parents and to make friends.

Iana Muntean, Moldova

CEACHT A HAON – AON BHLIAIN DÉAG

It's been 11 years now since I left my homeland, a land I hadn't left at all before at 20 years of age. Well, I had traveled to Portugal for a few days, but when you are from Spain, that does not really count as going abroad.

In any case, I came to Galway directly from my native town in 1996 and it was quite different than it is today. For example, I still remember the Glen Dara tower blocks that made me feel at home so much because they resembled the area in which my parents still live. I was here back then as one of the first Erasmus students from my city. You may have noticed how I am not giving its name. My reason is: I want to tell you just about my experience outside the place where I am from. This exercise of self-imposed exile has resulted in a flexibility I never expected my roots and/or my heart to have.

So in my memory Galway, then, in 1996 is an old city, with far less money that it shows off today. There were not so many cars though the bus service was as idiosyncratic and there were definitely fewer businesses. I remember that even though it was illegal to study and work at the same time[1], we all tried to look for a job quite unsuccessfully, whereas now... I am totally on the other side of the spectrum. Now I am a teacher at NUIG and I hear the Erasmus students from my own city choosing between jobs, complaining about getting an hourly rate that they would never dream of at home - granted they would never pay the rent they pay here back home either.

So yes, I live here now on the other side of the river, but I did not stay here for these 11 years. It's been only four since I returned. In between I put into practice the old chameleon nature and tried to blend in England, Brazil and finally Canada. It all went well. I learnt one of my lessons. I discovered how many people I could potentially become and indeed became in all these places, but it was not until I came back to Galway in 2003, now as a professional, and with a blooming career, right into the centre of a vibrant Galway, much more hybrid and rich in wealth and character... It was not until then I realized, when I started learning my bit of Irish, that they already knew it here, well before. Tá mé i mo chónaí i nGaillimh. They already knew I was about to change again into who I am now because I am living here, because I am interacting with the city, with the peoples and the land, because I am learning to see things again in a different way and to express them.

I will never be totally uprooted, I will never cease to be from where I am from, but now I've branched out and my fruits, like an overgrown tree, spread into your gardens, Eirinn. Hopefully your soil will be improved by all of us.

Irma Mento, Spain

¹ As illegal as the poteen we were offered on the very first night we arrived by the guardian angel of a guesthouse who took pity on two poor foreigners looking as lost as you possibly can on the platform because the student residence we were going to move into had just told us we could not move in until three days later even though we had started to pay 12 days before.

THE FORTRESS – AN IRISH EMIGRANT'S SON
BACK IN THE THICK OF IT

Is cuid me o ghlúin mo shinsereacht
I am a part of the generations of my ancestors
When I tell you I was born in Scotland you will call me Scottish
When I tell you I'm Irish you will still call me Scottish.
And who are you?
You say you are Cré na Cille
I am too.
Is Raghallaigh mé!
Blood line of Niall of the Nine Hostages
I am emigrant Irish,
You are Free State Irish.
I am of the 80 million
You are of the 4.
What happened amongst ye?
Awkward household of Survivors and Landlords' sons
Was the Civil War's triumph to cut off so many of us?
Is that why ye fenced off the Commonages?
Ye won't cut me off! Ye feckers!

My wandering accent has become like yours.
I could be like you –
But I won't!
No polite homogenous shuffle to receive.
I hate English!
I am losing it, you are gaining it
I love Irish!
I am gaining it, you are losing it.
I know the struggle.
You have forgotten war.
You pay an easy tribute
You are rewarded
In paper tits and Premiership balls.

Romanized Celts! Suckers!
You have become politically reliable.
But I do not fear we will be a lost land
Because of the Fortress.
Cu Chullain would marvel at your cars,
Yet he knew who the Romans were. His spear is raised towards you.
The locals, faintly Gaelic.
'Who are you?'
I have declared myself...you haven't.

What did Ye learn in the Famine?
Would you betray your liberators in the hope
That the Gombeen man will deliver you a victim?
A servant who will curse you.
I would not rush to lead you!
Ye still vote for those bastards!
Shape-shifters!
Ambitious young men become conformed to their sullen likeness.
The Visions perish, the Apparitions cease...
And another generation paddles its own canoe
To the toll-boom, where the Bailiff waits sneering.

But I know the Fortress will stand
Besieged by battalions of whores.
In the land of my conquerors I learned what it holds,
Unshielded and wincing before a cruel spear's point.
We, The Irish,
Though more English than the English themselves,
Still are not like them.

David O'Reilly, Galway

Ireland is a very fine country. I am happy to live here. Of course, not everything is perfect but I am happy to be here. I had big problems at home, and here you can forget all that and just have your life. I work hard and my wife too, to get all the things we want. I hear people complaining and I say to them: what is it you want then? I am here 5 years now and I feel like I am an Irishman now. The only thing I don't like here is the food. In the beginning when I am here first it was not easy to find food from Africa, but now there are many, many shops, you can buy whatever you want.

Galway is small very friendly town. My children have been born here in the hospitals, and I give them Irish names. I want them to be happy here, and be citizens of this country. On official level, I think everyone treats us in a very good, fair way. When I go to the City Hall, the officials are very respectful and do everything they can to help. They are good people. I have no complaint about that.

Sometimes you must be careful. A few years ago, I drove a taxi and then you can have a big problem, so many people are drinking. One night a man got into the taxi with his wife, he was very drunk and not very polite. He told me he can show me where to go. We drove for a long time, about 30 miles into the country. It was late at night. The road was very bad. When we got to his house he started to argue about how much to pay. It was on the taxi metre but he said no. I was afraid. People came out of the house and started to shout. But that was one time. Most times people are friendly and polite. In the school, my children are very happy. The teachers talk about our culture too, and they learn Irish language. I think that is a good thing, all the children play together and there is no problem.

There is one thing which is not so good. A couple of years ago I bought a piece of land. It is not big, but I wanted to build a house. But I cannot get the planning permission. I have talked to many people in the County Council and everywhere, and there is no explanation. I don't understand that. The land is mine, I have a right to build a house for my family, where they can live. I ask everyone but no one can explain. They say that no one can build on this land, but everywhere you see people building new houses. It seems strange to me that my land has no rights. I will keep trying. I know that someday I will build a house here for my children to live in.

Anonymous, Nigeria

THE SENSITIVITY OF WORDS

Filled with suspicion I am opening a new day. I am treading carefully in this malleable micro-world. One can transform it easily. The deformed reality. Quasi-existence. It is fading away in an abyss of a language which rubs away the contours of my identity. I am mute. The reflection of words, these mirrors for the thoughts not to be captured. Deep inside I scream in my own language, the words are approaching the throat and stopping on a surface of the space where the sound is being created. They revert to the depth and get tangled in an irriting dust of introversion. And then the trapped words drift into my throat again and here it is the eternity of recurrence. This is a wicked language. Like scratching on a polished glass surface. Like nails breaking. The pace is too fast. The vowels are fleeting before I am able to comprehend them. They are whirling as if they were soap bubbles. They are collapsing suddenly, however, imperceptibly. Beyond a day I experience alternative lives. Disturbing lives. Lives under metamorphoses. The tenebrous hallways of my soul. And once there was a dream. It drifted into the fragile frames of night-time. I found myself in a small room with a twinkling light. The space is shrinking violently. The crowd is moving violently around me. The paper walls are getting thinner, the whole room is swallowing me and I am becoming the room itself. Gasping for the luxury of a breath. What is left now, is what has been saved. Snatches of nothingness.

Kinga Cybulska, Poland

MY HUSBAND'S JOB EXPERIENCE IN GALWAY

My husband started work in a company one year ago. He was very happy to start working in an Irish Company and to be a part of a team. Plus the employer promised him a very good full time contract with good conditions and a well paid job. But those were promises.

Since he has started work he has found this company unstable. But he continued to trust his employer and problems with salary and working hours just as temporary things.

He tried to talk with his employer about this situation, but the employer just promised him.

After half year he understood that his employer exploited him. He with other employees started looking for a help in different organisations. Because of incorrect payments and late salary payments of 4-5 weeks, wrong tax deduction, unpaid holidays and travels and overtime as well.

Abuse and discrimination are policies of this company.

People came from different countries to Ireland (Galway) and hoped to work and be secure by law. But in real life during seven month they have not sorted out all the problems.

People have been really shocked because the boss of this company says to them (face to face) using bad language they are just foreign in this country and that the employer is an IRISH EMPLOYER and would not have any problem and is not afraid of anybody.

All employees of this company (they are all foreign people) have had a bad experience.

For my husband it is very hard to look at his children's eyes and explain to them why we do not have money to buy something for them, if their father works.

Anonymous, Russia

MY STORY

In 1952 I emigrated to America seeking employment, I was just nineteen. Times were hard in Ireland so many like me were seeking a better way of life.

I arrived in New York, a strange and foreign city, disembarking from the Cunard Liner The Franconia after ten days of sea sickness.

We lived in the Bronx. I had no trouble finding a job as a domestic.

Meeting my young man, marrying him, settling down, soon we were parents to two lovely sons. Our happiness was shattered with the sudden death of my young husband. I was left to rear my two boys.

I soon packed my bags and returned home to my mother in Galway. Our trip home was beautiful, travelling first class in the S.S. America, only five days on the ocean, no sea sickness.

Mother welcomed us with open arms into her little cottage in Ballybrit. My son Michael was in awe at seeing the range and a fire. He had never seen a fire before.

After all the conveniences of running water and domestic appliances, I had a rude awakening after the luxury of almost twelve years; I had many inconveniences to get used to.

Explaining the outdoor tiolet facilities to Michael he was highly amused by the slush bucket, and the scraps of torn newspapers hung on a nail at the back of the shed door, but he adapted quicly.

I din't! I needed a washing machine. Mam was very proud of having the electricity, switching it on for me to see. We didn't have that in 1952 when you left, about 1956 we got it in. A blessing for the wireless, her only luxury.

Buying a twin tub washing machine I thought was the answer to my laundry problems. Drawing water from the cattle drinking trough, heating it on top of the range, filling and emptying the twin tub manually, was a testing time for me that Mam took in her stride.

The pump for drinking water was a mile away, my son loved to swing from the handle while I pumped, carrying buckets of water blistered the palms of my hand. In the eleven and a half years I was away nothing had changed.

I updated my mode of transport by buying a green Mini Minor HIM 192 in 1964, people admired it, there were very few cars on the road back then. In their admiration for the Mini I would be asked how much I knew about a car. I'd answer 'I know how to check the water, dip the oil, change a wheel.' This was taught me by a mechanic who worked in O'Flaherty's garage on Fr. Griffin Road where I bought the Mini. He gave me three driving lessons and I went off on my own, in first and second gears. My £380 Mini Minor lasted me eight and a half years. The questions I was asked were more about engine capacity etc., which I didn't know so I got a knowing glance.

I moved to a thatched cottage in Ballyloughan. I bought a ¼ acre of ground in Ballybane for £430. An engineer, John Coyne, drew plans for a two storey house; he also supervised the building of the house. His price for a job well done was £34, he told me the day of the engineer drawing up plans was over. 'It's over to architects who will charge an arm and a leg,' he said.

The house was built within a year at a cost of £3,490 by Sean Usher Building Contractors.

Paddy McDermott R.I.P., moved my belongings in his ass and cart for £1. Now I had my home I could buy all the modern appliances I needed. It was 1965.

A great big water storage tank stood outside my kitchen window, a pump was installed in the kitchen to draw the water up to the attic tanks.

Doing B&B in Race Week was very busy. Jockeys and trainers were my biggest clients. They would sleep anywhere as long as they had a roof over them. No fuss about ensuites.

Then the water ran out, flushing toilets. I had five bedrooms accomodating 12 – 14 people.

Then I had to buy the water, £ 20 for a tank full. I was asked by several, why such a big house and you a widow, I was informed. I had the feeling that as a young widow I was answerable to people for what I took on. These questions I could never comprehend until one evening I was reading The Connacht Tribune, there was an article on the rights of women who in the workplace were not receiving equal pay with their male counterparts for the same work done.

I realised then that women here in Ireland were very much treated as second-class citizens. What was being said to me all along were not compliments, but more in criticism.

It's 2008. I'm still here, my big house sold now. In its place modern day apartments, my two sons who received top education in the schools and colleges of Galway returned to their birthland, the USA.

Margaret Dowling, Galway

LISTENING TO IRISH SONGS

What they do to us, these songs
The ballads of Transylvanian Gypsies
Tangos, fados, Georgian laments -
The music speaks to us in words
We cannot understand, except for one or two
Perhaps, stepping stones which lead us over
A river of black emotion.

Like these Irish songs I hear in pubs
Or on the local radio. Some words
I have learned to recognize,
Like *Muir* for the sea. That's an easy one
Cognate with Romance languages.
Then there's *croí*, for heart. That's harder
But still not far from *coeur* and *corazon*.
But what about words like *brón* and *uaigneas*?
And my favourite, the word for red: *dearg*
Strange and contingent as our Latvian *sarkans*...

Do I need to learn this language to understand
The songs? No.
Sea and heart, sorrow and red,
The story is always the same.

Like that girl who works in the corner shop
Where I buy my cigarettes.
I don't know her name or nation
But her eyes are a country which invites
Me to explore its hinterland.
Every day we talk until
I stop and she stops, and she smiles
And waits on the threshold
While I look into those bogholes, thinking:
At the centre of every eye
A circle of blackness, the same
In every woman I've ever loved
And then I say goodbye and turn away.

Mikelis Norgelis, Latvia

BACK HOME TO IRELAND

I was just seven years old when we moved 'back home to Ireland' from Coventry in the English West Midlands during the summer of 1974. These days, when I remember Coventry, the pictures come in full colour: our 'hippie' teacher, who sang Joni Mitchell songs and told us the meaning of big words, such as 'hypocrite'; my teddy-bear 'Sooty', lost forever during a train-journey to Luton; the day I saw a worm wriggling up through the soil in our back garden and ran in screaming, telling my mother I'd seen a snake! And, of course, television. *The Magic Roundabout* and *Basil Brush*. *Dr. Who and the Daleks*: 'Exterminate! Exterminate!'

In the adult world these where times of upheaval. There were power-cuts as the miners went on strike, not once but twice. It also saw the beginning of the IRA bombing campaign in Britain. A man was blown up by his own bomb at the nearby telephone exchange. I remember my father playing James Connolly and other rebel songs on the record player with the volume turned up full blast. But the closest this ugly adult stuff came to intruding on my small reality was when as episode of Basil Brush was cancelled to facilitate coverage of the February 1974 General Election. I remember indignantly asking my mother who 'those two Prime Minister men were?' She informed me that one of them was Ted Heath, the other Harold Wilson and suggested that I go outside and play.

I remember crying during dinnertime on my last day at school at The Sacred Heart on Harefield Road and being comforted by one of the girls in the class. It wasn't that I particularly liked school, more that, on some instinctive level, I could sense that this relatively happy chapter of my life was drawing to a close. The following Saturday we packed our belongings into a huge removal van and hit the motorway for Holyhead.

The pictures I have of Galway during the mid-nineteen seventies are all in black and white. I remember turning the television on, one afternoon, because it was time for *Sooty and Sweep*, but there

Saskia Bekova, Czech Republic

IMPRESSIONS OF GALWAY

It was a bright sunny November day, when we arrived to Galway. It was a surprise, because we thought that in Ireland it never stops raining... So we took this as a good omen for the start of a new life in a new city!

At first we wanted to see the coast. Those who live in a country where the largest lake's average depth is 3 m, really can appreciate this mightiness of nature. Locals perhaps get used to the sight, the scent and the sound of the ocean. But we simply loved it. Now, several months later we also get used to it... It's human nature. We always have to remind ourselves to spot the beauty of everyday life.

I can't avoid to mention the glamorous rainbows I've seen here! Thanks to the rain... If I were the first human to ever discover this city, I would definitely call it the City of Rainbows.

In the next few weeks we had occasion to experience the ´beauty´of the Irish weather... The variety of the rain was inexhaustible: drizzle, spit, hail, sleet, snow, all these combined with wind, vertical rain, horizontal rain, diagonal rain, rain from every side. We mostly used bikes as a vehicle so it was a tough period for us. Physically, mentally and spiritually. Really... But we survived.

During the winter here, I was completly astonished to see guys in shorts, women wearing little summer dresses with sandals, shaking like icecubes! I know fashion is important, but for god's sake, being blue is not trendy! Or is it?

Returning to the smoking... As a smoker I find it very uncomfortable to smoke outside in the cold. I totally understand and accept the necessity of this law concerning the non-smokers... but I still find it a bit discriminatory. I am sure that if this decision were be enacted in my country it would probably raise a kind of 'smokers revolution'... or at least a demonstration.

There are loads of adorable things here: the cute little pubs, the ambience of trad sessions, the cultural movement, the bohemian look of the streets of the centre, the low houses with tiny windows, the

colorful doors, the riverside, the bay with swans, seagulls and ducks...
And of course you, Galwegians.

All the Irish people I met in this city were very nice and welcoming
to me. When you talk you are disarming and cheerful. When you are
in traffic you are tolerant and relaxed. When you drive your car you
don't really pay attention to the cyclists and you drive into a big puddle
and get everyone around soaked. When you employ you are fair and
patient. When you cook, well, it's flavourless, you don't use spices and
salt. When you drink, you drink too much and become straggling
(after a Saturday night rip-roaring I found quite a lot of things on
Eyre Square, e.g. mobile phones, wallets, etc.) and you break too many
bottles. When you are a teenager, you think you are the centre of the
world and don't respect others and your own town. And when you are
an adult, you are a bit too permissive with the teenagers...

But in spite of these things I found you a very friendly folk. And I
think Galway is a stunning city to live in. I'm glad to be here.

Viktoria Katona, Hungary

MY STORY OF GALWAY

When I came to Ireland I was very happy because that was the first year when I get married and visited Ireland, the first year I lived in Cavan it was a small city and small population with different culture.

I didn't know anybody spoke like me and I didn't speak English at all, I know just simple words, sometimes when I would like to go outside I need time to take a decision what I have to do (stay at home or go outside). It was a difficult decision because if I stay at home I feel bored, or if I go out I feel afraid.

The people looked at me like I was strange, I felt like some one come from another world.

I wore a scarf on my head, the people stared at me, I felt that in their eyes, when the people looked at me like that I didn't feel good and I can't go outside again, to forget what happened, I need more time to do that again.

One year later my daughter was born, nobody with me, I cannot go with her anywhere, I'm always at home, sometimes I would like to walk or go to the park or shopping with her but I feel nervous and scared.

I couldn't push myself to learn English or make relationships with my neighbours because I can't communicate with them without English.

Every year I have to move from city to city according to my husband's work and I didn't stay in the same house for long, at last after four years I came to Galway.

I am here approximately three years, I did many things in this city which was good experience for me, I learned English, made friends, I feel more confident than before, I am not afraid, I don't care about the language, I try to speak and try to understand.

I think it was like a challenge to myself to adapt to this new situation.

Lastly, living in Galway is one of the best experience in my life with a lot of knowledge and training experience.

I would like to say thanks for my husband who supports me and for the teachers in my school.

As a result we found the old Galway shops and especially the clothes shops extremely expensive and offering very little choice. And money was beginning to get scarce. In America I had earned approximately $250 weekly, which at the time was the equivalent of £80 and with overtime this could rise to £100, a large amount in the 1960s.

In Galway my salary was £40 monthly – £10 weekly with overtime unpaid, so whenever I or my friends wanted to replenish our wardrobes, we'd head for Dublin.

In those days too, all the Galway shops closed on Monday leaving the city looking like a ghost town. And on top of everything else, all the dances ended at midnight, an hour at which in Cork and Dublin everything would be beginning to liven up. By half past eleven Galway was quiet, the streets dark and deserted. The pubs and cinemas were closed and the only places still showing any signs of life were the three dance halls – Seapoint, The Hangar and The Talk of the Town. By half past twelve these too were dark and silent. These are the things I found disappointing about Galway. There was much that I found unique and charming, the lovely smell that hung like a veil over the city and suburbs, the fields behind the houses on Woodquay and Bohermore now all built on. But then cattle grazed there and hens ducks and geese roamed free and this the very heart of the city.

When I had been working in Galway for two years I married my husband, a farmer and moved to the new house he had built on the farm which although only five miles from Galway, at that time was in the middle of the country. I who am city born and bred found it very remote and lonely.

At the time when our house was built there was no water scheme in our area- my husband was one of the people responsible for getting the scheme up and running about three years later. In the meantime we had a huge concrete underground tank which held three thousand gallons and was fed by pipes which carried rainwater from the roofs of the house and the outbuildings.

As we couldn't drink this water we had to make two or three trips daily to the communal spring water tap situated about a mile from our house. Even though we made the trip by car, it was still an inconvenience, especially with young children.

Because of our water situation I was unable to have an automatic washing machine which I really wanted, but had to be content with a twin tub. But I really didn't really mind, it was a happy time for us.

In summer, during the hot dry weather, we had to buy water. A man whose name I have forgotten had a horse drawn cart with a huge oil container which he filled from Lough Corrib, would come and fill our tank and those of our neighbours. Because our tank was so big he needed several trips to fill it. For this he charged £10. At one stage he was coming to us every six weeks. On one visit to me he said "Hey Mrs, you better tell your husband there's a leak in that tank. There's no way such a big tank would need to be filled so often. I don't mind," he continued "It's all money in my pocket, but it's not fair on ye". He was an honest man. So I told my husband we had a leak in our tank. "We've no leak, Catherine" he replied, "it's you and the children having baths every day and all the washing you're doing". So we kept on buying water until we got the group water scheme. Now of course we're connected to the city water supply.

Galway has changed beyond all recognition in the forty years I've been here. Gone is the old grey city by the sea, replaced by a busy modern town that has tripled in size. The old stone houses have been restored, many of them turned into restaurants, boutiques, fashionable pubs for young people and antique and souvenir shops. Where the grim warehouses once stood are modern apartment buildings and hotels. Most of them I think, in keeping with the ethos of this old historic city. Almost all the old shops have been replaced by multinational chain stores, which is a pity, but it keeps prices down, so we don't complain.

And Galway no longer closes down at midnight. In fact it is now the liveliest of all Ireland's cities, keeping going day and night and never seems to close down at all. Visitors, especially young people flock here all the year round. But unfortunately crime, almost non existent in the old city is now an increasingly worrying problem. And I no longer live in the middle of the country, our area is fast becoming a suburb of Galway. We can no longer walk safely on the lovely roads around our house, once so quiet but now filled with a constant stream of cars and lorries rushing past.

When I got married this was an Irish speaking area, now sadly Irish has faded out. Although the older people are fluent in our native tongue, they never speak it now. Large houses have been built on the fields around us. Every house including our own with two, three or more cars. There are fewer cattle in the fields now but it's good to see an increasing number of horses. Not of course the working horses of forty years ago, but thoroughbreds, hunters and Connemara ponies for the children to ride. All proclaiming our new wealthy status.

And what of Connemara? That place of beauty and poverty. Where in the sixties donkeys laden with baskets of turf plodded home to small white washed thatched houses. Where in many parts people were still unable to speak English. A place for the most part undiscovered by people from the rest of Ireland. Connemara has become a place of luxury houses, golf courses, expensive hotels and restaurants catering for every taste. Where many government members, film actors, writers and pop stars have holiday homes.

Where the only thatched houses to be seen now are more suited to an English tourist village than to that wild mountainous coast. Thankfully Irish is still spoken in most parts of Connemara and spoken with pride by a cultured educated generation.

Every summer large numbers of school children and young people come here to learn to speak "proper" Irish. As opposed to the Anglicised version taught in most schools. I think Connemara has seen the greatest changes of all. Galway admittedly was a much poorer place forty years ago, but I wonder sometimes if with all here present, wealth and advantages, has she last her soul?

Catherine Corcoran, Galway

KALEIDOSCOPE

The rainbow formed from car fumes and sunshine
is setting onto a cut-out
At the corner of Moulin Rouge in a marshmallow factory
Mosquitoes are copulating
Lady cellophane drinks a coffee from a polystyrene cup
in the street where the butcher's stands and rosebuds are dead

A butterfly lost in a green puddle
Is weighing its shadow
metamorphosing into an unreal relic to me

A lord of polyphonic identity is a split ends' enthusiast
With a fluorescent wig made of hyperactive staccato sounds

A mindmap is a zigzag of shooting stars
And each piece of chocolate has its own motto
Like a mouth full of teeth
Every single one from a different smile

Joanna Chodan, Poland

LIVING IN GALWAY

I think Galway is a good place to live. I have lived here for eight years now. I have seen many, many changes. At the beginning there were not so many Africans at all here. When more Africans came people thought we are all from the same country, even the same town. I told people all the time that in my country we speak French. It was a French colony. This was surprising for many people. They did not know where Togo was until the World Cup in 2006! Then everybody knew it. But I always say to people, this. All of Africa is a colony, that is why I am here!

I think that Irish people understand very well this history because your history is like it. Ireland was a colony too. The other good thing in Galway is the community. The people in Galway are a community, there are many people who work hard for the community. That is good. I lived in Paris too, there is no community there.

Now there are many Africans here, from many countries. That is a big change. We are the same in some things but I have to explain also the differences between West Africa and East Africa, the food, the clothes, the languages, everything is different. But we are all Africa, of course.

Another big change is the dirty streets. When I was here then, everywhere you saw plastic bags lying around. Now it is much cleaner, I like that. Also Galway is a great place now to listen to music, there is music everwhere, Irish music, African music, every kind. There are so many musicians living here, even when I walk down the street I hear different kinds.

Galway people are friendly, but they always complain. They complain a lot about politicians., that they are bad men, only for themselves, that they are corrupt. I say to them, yes maybe they are corrupt, but only a little bit, you should be glad!

I love everything in Galway except one thing, I am sorry to say it, the weather. It is so depressing. I think that if Galway has the African sun here, then Galway is a perfect place for me!

Nicolas, Togo

THE BIG BANG

Suddenly, the large street became smaller, almost a tiny asphalt line. Houses nearby had grown and with big eyes stared at me. The air was thick and made my breath awful as if I was inhaling something caustic. A cloud had blackened the sky.

At the rear of my car, traffic that was already heavy became worse, now stopped. Drivers looked at me with angry faces...

My brain was trying to understand what was happening. But it wasn't easy. I stood outside, on the edge of the road. Insurance contract in my hand. I had already tried to speak with the other two drivers involved in this traffic accident. They hadn't even noticed me.

The middle age women who owned the car in front of mine only sighed, showing a painful expression. From the third car two children had left and now were playing on the footpath. A fat man, I assumed the driver, was outside too, near the wife who was on the phone. Only after she had finished the call, she picked up a newborn from the rear seat...

I entered my car again.

"What the hell is happening here?"

"What are they waiting for?"

"What are they trying to do?"

My English/Irish friend Joanne, also astonished, answered:

"I suppose they have called the Gardai!"

"They are going to say that this is all your fault"

"And really, the car that you have touched has no damage! And neither does our car!"

"The Gardai, because of this?" I replied slowly, as if I was eating the words. My son and her daughter, as soon they heard about "Gardai" started asking us: "Are we going to jail?"

My hands were shaking, truly all my body was shaking. Not because of this ordinary accident, but because of a behaviour that I couldn't understand.

Forty minutes later, a Garda car appeared, siren on, driving on the wrong side of the road.

Another car parked near us. A young woman ran to the one who continued sighing.

Then, the scenario became even worse. The policeman was surrounded by the Irish people. They were speaking loudly, they were gesticulating a lot, they were pointing at me.

I heard "It was a big bang!" "She hadn't said she was sorry!"

I began shaking even more, now I was very mad. I wished to be a wrestling fighter and pick up all of them in the air and make them spin, as we see in those funny combats, on TV.

The Garda rudely approached me:

"You were driving too fast and provoked this mess!"

"Oh yeah! We can see that! We haven't done any damage! The damage was between the two other cars!" Joanne replied to him.

At the time, my head seemed unable to process English words but I managed:

"Nobody is hurt, I am legal, my car is legal, I have insurance...why so the raw deal?"

The policeman melted a little. He took my driving license and my insurance contract.

"Sorry, but you need to come with me to the police station. I need copies."

"Park your car next to mine, I will stop the traffic."

I was relieved because finally this mess would at last end.

Another Garda car stopped near us!

Another man approached!

All stood there, talking, talking...

After three hours, all this incident was left behind. It is not easy to forget the xenophobic behaviour. I imagine if I was colored ... This attitude shows the worst kind of violence: to judge and condemn without hearing or saying a word.

As my husband had lately said to me: "Stupid people can be found everywhere", and the best thing is to insult them in Portuguese, with a smile on our face. That way our stress comes out!

Ana Quaresma, Portugal

MY EXPERIENCE IN GALWAY

When I arrived in Galway, I didn't speak English, only a few words, even though my first impression of the city was great and the first few days were sunny, I felt upset because it wasn't easy for me to talk with the people. The worst thing for me was to speak on the phone because the people could not realize that I didn't speak English.

Soon I noticed that it was easier than what I thought. People were kind and whenever they saw I wasn't a fluent English speaker they made an effort to communicate with me.

It is amazing the amount of people speaking different languages living in Galway and everyone learning English to try to communicate with each other.

Agustina Marreins, Argentina

FROM AHAB'S LOG BOOK FEBRUARY 2002

For weeks the sea lay dozing like a cat
but three nights ago it turned over
shook its mane and rose up hissing
along the foreshore of Black Head.

Somewhere lost within its belly
tumbles my white whale,
small and luminous as a firefly.
I sailed into this westernmost town

at the dark edge of Europe
to shelter from the never-ending gales,
moored the *Pequod*
alongside a wrecked stone pier

and limped into the centre
of what seems to be a place
entirely preoccupied with holiness –
church spires, bells and convents everywhere

and since it was Ash Wednesday
the foreheads of the entire populace
were streaked with grey.
Their drink is the colour and smell of soutanes,

which must be some local
form of penance,
all streets have saints' names
and no doubt lead straight to heaven.

I bide my time in a sandwich bar
beside the tackle shop
and listen to a street musician strain
the mournful air through harp strings.

Having found a companion
in a wild-haired old man, a sailor
who claims to have lost his ship and crew
somewhere in the mountains of Armenia,

we solve riddles together, anagrams,
I ask him what kept Ishmael afloat
after the Pequod sank:
a coffin, a barrel of oil, a lifeboat, a mattress?

he asks me what I saw
in the gold doubloon I nailed to the mast:
myself, God,
the face of evil?

This is how we pass the night
while the storm clatters
on its typewriter
above the hostelry roof.

The terraced houses lie in wait
linking arms.
If they abide long enough
they might witness the showdown.

All paths leading to the water
are empty.
The hours last
as never before.

I can expect little from the sky
from which darkness hangs
like a saw-toothed star,
a poem dictated to the night in a boarded-up room.

Eva Bourke, Germany

I came to Galway because my cousin lives here and he loves it. It's a real fun town. When I came here everyone was very helpful and made me feel at home but I wasn't really happy for a long time. For me the big problem was the English language. I speak ok English now but it was not easy to start. There are many Polish people here so you can always talk to someone, but that is not a situation to be completely part of that group.

But the problem was bigger. In Poland I studied economics and did a Masters Degree at university. I want to use my degree but without English that was difficult to start. In Poland I worked in a bank but that was not possible here. I worked at different jobs, in bars and cafes. It was not so bad and the pay is good. However, that was not what I wanted. I think there are a lot of highly qualified Polish people, doctors and nurses, people with PhDs, who are in Ireland but would like to get a job at their own specialty. That is good for Ireland and for us!

Really it took me a few years to feel comfortable with English. Now I can speak it well I think, so I am more confident in looking for jobs. I have a job now in an office and that is very good, answering the phone, even writing letters. I feel it has a possibility of improving. My ambition is to work in the bank.

In the beginning the cultural differences were important to me but now I see that they are not so big. In fact, Ireland and Poland are very similar in many ways. For examples, family values are important for us both, Polish and Irish. The food is also not so different. The main cultural differences are in little things. For example, I have been invited to many weddings here in Ireland, with Irish people. It's a little shocking that the bar is not free, and people have to buy their own drinks. At a wedding in Poland, everything is free. But these are small things.

I like to dance, and there is good places for that in Galway. But it was shocking to see how young people, some of them very young, were drinking till they fell down. In Poland we drink too, but you cannot see that behaviour in the pubs. For me the important thing about Galway now is that this is where I met my husband! He is Irish, and from the beginning there was not a problem with our language. He is learning a little Polish now, so that when he visits my family in Poland he can talk to people. But living with him makes my English improve a lot faster!

There are so many things I love now in Galway, I love the sea for example, and walking along the Prom in Salthill. I would miss that in my town in Poland. In the Summer there's a great atmosphere with all the festivals and people. Galway is home for me now. The only problem is the weather. In Poland it's hot in summer and cold in winter, much colder than Galway. But I never felt so cold as here in Galway in the winter, it's wet and miserable!

But all that is not so important. I have a beautiful house now in Galway, and a job, so I am going to stay here. I'm a Galwegian too now!

Anna Baraczek, Poland

FIND GALWAY, CIRCA 1985

Look up, the wind could be stronger. See the gargoyles on Lynch's Castle and St. Nick's, see how the railings around the church are the perfect height to lean against and see the goth-black boys, their long lcoats like wings in the wind of mid-December, follow them up to Brambles Café, past McCambridges (closed because it's lunchtime) and did you know McCambridges sells the only bottle of Heinz ketchup in town, or that the Square turns into Williamsgate Street turns into Shop Street turns into Mainguard Street or High Street depending on the way you go? Ask me where river ends and tide begins. Ask me the name of the city councillor who voted against nudity, the shop that takes butter vouchers for cigarettes. These are the subtleties I have learned: that to pass the time of day means to stop for the moment it takes to dissect the weather with someone you have met at least once. How a good hood works better than an umbrella in these medieval-sized streets, and the way the cars have to stop for you – it's a Galway law – and you cross the road whenever you need to, higgledy-piggledy, to get to O'Brien's for the news, to give a wide berth to Una's dogs and the cars that are trying to avoid these tails and do you know the exact point where Dennis harasses the tourists and Elvis sings for me, never falling off his bike, right there where Williamsgate Street turns into Shop Street; and you keep going, on past Holland's and Deacy's and McDonagh's, past the fresh fish and the vision of future pints outside the Quays on a rare warm night, keep going down past the Spanish Arch, the Basin, the Long Walk, out to the pull of salt and look I am thirteen, one year here, I am the water, I am the blackweed tangled up by the tides, I am pulled by the tides, a foreign body obeying the tug of the moon, I am the rough thin strip of sand left, I am the stink of rotting seaweed and sewage, I am faster than the walk out to Mutton Island, I am spring tides washing ashore the city's flotsam: Supermacs bags, illicit condoms, jobless blocklayers, dreamers.

I am Galway.

Celeste Augé, Galway

Michael O'Loughlin was born in Dublin in 1958 and studied at Trinity College Dublin.

His poetry collections are *Stalingrad: The Street Dictionary* (Dublin, Raven Press, 1980); *Atlantic Blues* (Dublin, Raven Arts Press, 1982); *The Diary of a Silence* (Raven Arts Press, 1985); and *Another Nation, New and Selected Poems* (Dublin, New Island Books, 1994/UK Arc Publications, 1996).

He has also published a collection of short stories, *The Inside Story* (Raven Arts Press, 1999); a critical essay, *After Kavanagh: Patrick Kavanagh and the Discourse of Contemporary Irish Poetry* (Raven Arts Press, 1985); and his translation of the Dutch poet Gerrit Achterberg's selected poems, *Hidden Weddings* (Raven Arts Press, 1987). He has also written screenplays for three feature films, most recently *Snapshots* (First Look Home Entertainment, 2003).

He lived for many years in Amsterdam and since 2006 he has been Writer in Residence for Galway City Council.